Revised 2nd Edition

The Last Help
Before
The End of Time
The Ultimate
Message of Fatima

Revised 2nd Edition

The Last Help Before The End of Time

The Ultimate Message of Fatima

Prof. Courtenay Bartholomew, M.D.

Queenship
Publishing Company

Library of Congress Number #2005905473

First Printing 2005
Second Printing 2006 Revised Edition

Published by:

Queenship Publishing Company Inc.
P.O. Box 220 • Goleta, CA 93116
(800) 647-9882 • (805) 692-0043
www.queenship.org

Printed in the United States of America

ISBN: 1-57918-320-4

IMPRIMATUR:

The Most Reverend Edward J. Gilbert, C.Ss.R.
Archbishop of Port of Spain
November 17, 2004

The Last Help Before The End Of Time

In Memory

of

Mlle Berthe Petit
(1870-1943)

"The title of **'Immaculate'** belongs to the whole being of My mother and not specially to her Heart. This title flows from my gratuitous gift to the Virgin who was to give Me birth. My mother has acquired for her Heart the title of 'Sorrowful' by sharing generously in all the sufferings of My Heart and My Body from the crib to the Cross. There is not one of these Sorrows which did not pierce the Heart of My mother. Living image of My crucified Body, her virginal flesh bore the invisible marks of My wounds as her Heart felt the Sorrows of My own. Nothing could ever tarnish the incorruptibility of her Immaculate Heart.

"The title of **'Sorrowful'** belongs therefore to the Heart of My mother, and more than any other, this title is dear to her because it springs from the union of her Heart with Mine in the redemption of humanity. This title has been acquired by her through her full participation in My Calvary, and it precedes the gratuitous title 'Immaculate' which My love bestowed upon her by a singular privilege."

Jesus to Berthe Petit, 1920.

"My apostle will arise at the predestined hour when the appalling cataclysm which approaches will have upset all the present calculations of mankind and their deplorable policies. My will concerning My mother's glory will not be fulfilled at present."

Jesus to Berthe Petit, 1922

"Recourse to My mother under the title and invocation I wish for her universally, 'Sorrowful and Immaculate Heart of Mary, pray for us,' is the last help I shall give before the end of time."

Jesus to Berthe Petit,
1940

TABLE OF CONTENTS

Introduction

The first and undoubtedly the greatest and most terrible war in creation history took place in the empyrean heavens after which one third of the countless angelic corps and their leader Lucifer were thrust down to Earth. As Jesus testified : "I saw Satan fall like lightening from heaven" (Luke 10:18). Those fallen angelic spirits are roaming the earth and we are wrestling not against flesh and blood, but against the rulers of the world of darkness, against the spirits of wickedness in the high places (Eph.6:12). It is a battle for souls but this is so little appreciated by the world!

Now, wars were rife even in Old Testament times but the World Wars of 1914-1918 and 1939-1945 have introduced a note of savagery that men had thought belonged only to primitive times of the past. The plethora of ideological disputes, the monstrous destructiveness of modern weapons, and the great number of individuals involved have produced numbers of casualties that dwarf the carnage in the days of the barbarian invasions in Europe. In round figures the military dead of World War I totalled nearly 10 million plus more than 29 million wounded and missing and the estimated deaths in World War II were about 55 million.

World War II ended in August 1945 with the dropping of the atomic bomb in Hiroshima and Nagasaki. Planning began in March 1944 for the full-scale test of the atomic bomb. According to Richard Rhodes in his book *The Atomic Bomb*, when eventually it was tested, night was turned into day in spite of the very dark glasses the observers were wearing. Physicist George Kistiakowsky exclaimed: "I am sure that the end of the world, in the last millisecond of the earth's existence, the last man will see what we have just seen." Indeed, in the book *The Final Warning. The Legacy of Chernobyl,* Dr. Robert Hauser wrote: "Already there is concern that science has gone too far, that in splitting the atom man has crossed a threshold that threatens us all."

When on August 6, 1945, the first bomb was dropped on Hiroshima, people exposed within a half mile of the fire ball were seared to bundles of smoking black char in a fraction of a second as their internal organs boiled away. In the testimony of the survivors, they described ghastly scenes of people whose skin hung from them "like a kimono" and who plunged themselves into the rivers, shrieking in pain. Nearly 100,000 died instantly. On August 9, 1945, the second bomb fell on Nagasaki. Seventy thousand people died immediately. "We have done the devil's work," exclaimed Robert Oppenheimer soon afterwards. Indeed, he wondered whether the dead of Hiroshima and Nagasaki were not more fortunate than the survivors whose exposure to the bomb would have lifetime effects.

According to Rhodes, Robert Oppenheimer, the Director of the Manhattan project, did not doubt that he would be remembered to some degree and reviled as a man who led the work of bringing to mankind for the first time in its history the means of its own destruction. As Oppenheimer himself said: "After the blast, we knew the world would not be the same. A few people laughed, a few people cried. Most people were silent. I remembered the line from the Hindu scripture: 'Now I have become death, the destroyer of worlds.' I suppose all of us thought that one way or the other."

Leo Szilard, the emigré Hungarian theoretical physicist

and co-inventor of the nuclear reactor, was one of the scientists who also felt a measure of guilt for the development of such a terrible weapon of war: "The development of atomic power," he said "would provide the nations with a new means of destruction. The atomic bombs at our disposal represent only the first step in this direction and there is almost no limit to the destructive power which will become available in the course of their further development."

Since then several nations have joined the "nuclear club," including in more recent times, India, Pakistan and North Korea with Iran lying in the waiting room of the production line, threatening to wipe Israel off the face of the map of the world. There are now more than 50,000 nuclear warheads in the world with an explosive yield of 20 billion tons of TNT, roughly 2 million times the yield of the bomb that destroyed Hiroshima. Undoubtedly, the proliferation of nuclear weapons increases the risks of nuclear war and each year also increases the odds that a nation with irresponsible leaders or an unstable government will acquire nuclear arms with motives ranging from self preservation to religious fanaticism to justify a nuclear strike. As Hans Bethe, a theoretical physicist, one of the members of the scientific team who developed the bomb, said years later: "We thought we could control the genie. It wouldn't go into the bottle. But there were reasonable grounds for thinking we could contain it. I know now that this was an illusion."

The final statement from Vatican Council II, which was chaired by Pope Paul VI, included this remark: "Unless animosity and hatred are put aside and firm, honest agreements about world peace are concluded, humanity may, in spite of the wonders of modern science, go from the grave crisis of the present day to that dismal hour when the only peace it will experience will be the dreaded peace of death." Since that warning aggressive world politics, ethnic conflicts and religious fanaticism have escalated manyfold and world peace appears to be decades away. However, before she died in 1918, Jacinta, one of the little visionaries of Fatima, told her fellow seer Lucia: "Let them (the world) ask for peace through the *Immaculate Heart of Mary* for **God has entrusted the peace of the world to her."** It is the assignment and privilege He has given to His mother for being His companion from the crib to the Cross — for being His co-redemptrix.

This book tells the story of the messages of Our Lord to a chosen soul, Berthe Petit, through whom, just before and during World War I and World War II, He asked for the consecration of the whole world to the *Sorrowful and Immaculate Heart of Mary.* However, the time was not considered opportune by Rome and Jesus later added: "My apostle will arise at the predestined hour when the appalling cataclysm which approaches will have upset all the present calculations of mankind and their policies. My will concerning My mother's glory will not be fulfilled at present."

The prophecy was made in 1922 after the end of World War I and when mankind at that time had not foreseen the possibility of the creation of a nuclear bomb. But we now live in the age, not only of guided nuclear missiles, but also of misguided men, with the possibility of an "appalling cataclysm" to come. But it can all be prevented or at least lessened if we appeal to and invoke the intercession of the **Sorrowful and Immaculate Heart** of the Mother of God and the Queen of Peace.

"It is as a Son that I have conceived this devotion for My mother. It is as God I impose it."

Jesus to Berthe Petit, 1943

The Last Help Before The End Of Time

Chapter

1

On Private Revelations

The New Testament is a book of only a few thousand words and that is why the last verse in the Gospel of John reads: "There were many other things that Jesus did (and said); if all were written down, the world itself, I suppose, will not hold all the books which would have to be written" (John 21:25). And so, while God speaks to us first and foremost through the Holy Scriptures, he also speaks through the teachings of the Church and also through private revelations.

Indeed, in my opinion, the statement that is recited repeatedly in theological circles and scriptural discussions that "no Catholic is obligated by the Church to believe in any private revelation, the reason being that private revelations do not constitute part of the original Deposit of Faith, the official public revelation given to the Church which was closed with the death of the last of the apostles, John the Evangelist," tends to diminish significantly the great importance of the private revelations of Our Lord and His Mother. Surely, God has not ceased talking to us since the death of St. John nearly 2,000 years ago!

So said, it is significant that even in the new *Catechism*

of the Catholic Church, Article 1, 67, under the headline *There will be no further Revelations,* the only two paragraphs devoted to private revelations are in very small print in the size below:

> "Throughout the ages, there have been so-called 'private' revelations, some of which have been recognized by the authority of the Church. They do not belong, however, to the deposit of faith. It is not their role to improve or complete Christ's definitive Revelations, but to help live more fully by it in a certain period of history. The Magisterium of the Church, the *sensus fidelium,* knows how to discern and welcome in these revelations whatever constitutes an authentic call of Christ or his saints to the Church."

Yet three dogmas of the Church, which Catholics are obliged to believe, are not found in Sacred Scripture but have been the result of sound theological reasoning and supported by private revelation. For example, the dogma of the Perpetual Virginity of the Blessed Virgin Mary, the dogma of the Immaculate Conception of the Blessed Virgin Mary and the dogma of the bodily Assumption of the Blessed Virgin Mary have all been confirmed by Our Lady herself in her Church-approved apparitions in Guadalupe, Mexico in 1531, Lourdes, France in 1858 and at the Rue du Bac apparitions in Paris in 1830 respectively. Indeed, were it not for private revelation there would be no recitation of the Rosary, considered by many Catholics to be the most important prayer after the *Our Father,* no scapular devotion nor wearing of the sacramental, the Miraculous Medal (the Medal of the Immaculate Conception).

Fr. Albert Hebert, S.M., a Marist, in his book *The Tears of Mary and Fatima,* commented on some of the difficulties that are frequently associated with private revelations. He wrote: "It would appear that not all private revelations achieve their stated purpose. It would seem that some suffer so much harassment, interference and opposition from various sources, including, if not especially the clergy, that it is reasonable to believe that Christ or Mary would have to withdraw their own activity and influence at the site and terminate their mission." Indeed, Christ Himself once told His apostles when a city or town would not receive them, to shake the dust off their feet and go elsewhere (Matthew 10:14).

According to Fr. Hebert, it is also well known that "there have been persons, even the clergy, who in all sincerity meant well, but lacking full knowledge, experienced investigative abilities, intelligence and/or courage, or all of these qualities (or who may even be biased for one reason or the other) have caused great loss of grace and other supernatural favours from God. In fact, Our Lady of Fatima was so displeased with the harassment meted out to the child seers by the civil authority that she worked a lesser miracle than she had planned for October 13, 1917. As she said: "If they had not taken you to the town" (to prevent you from going to the apparition site on August 13), the miracle would be even greater."

Writing about the opposition which the three young visionaries in Fatima faced, he also mentioned the reluctance of one of the highest prelates in the Church hierarchy: "To spare his name, a certain Cardinal in Europe at one time forbade his priests to go to Fatima under pain of excommunication." However, the renowned Mariologist Fr. Robert J. Fox in his book *Fatima Today* did mention a name. "His Eminence, the

Cardinal Patriarch of Lisbon, Dom Antonio Mendes Bello," he wrote, "once prohibited the clergy from encouraging or taking part in any religious manifestation relating to Fatima." John Haffert, that great American apostle of Fatima, who first brought the devotion of Our Lady of Fatima to America, also once told me that the Cardinal repented on his death bed.

"There are similar instances in the history of genuine apparitions, stigmatists, saints, seers and/or holy persons," wrote Fr. Hebert. "In earlier years St. Joan of Arc was charged with heresy and witchcraft before the ecclesiastical court of Bishop Pierre Cauchon. Her visions were declared to be of diabolical origin and she was burnt at the stake on May 30, 1431. However, Pope Callistus III later appointed a court that found Joan innocent in 1456 and she was canonized in 1920 by Pope Benedict XV. In our own days the private revelations of Sr. Faustina of Poland were kept under wraps (by the bishops) for years. Sr. Faustina started her diary in 1938 and it was later condemned by the Congregation for the Doctrine of the Faith. However, in its revision in 1978, the Sacred Congregation withdrew the condemnation and reservations advanced earlier by the Holy See. Her 'Divine Mercy' messages and cult were later approved by a decree of April 15, 1987, influenced by Pope John Paul II when he was a Cardinal in Poland. Now her life, private revelations and the devotional literature on the Divine Mercy are being spread all over the world.

"As another example, although he was endowed with unusual mystical gifts and the stigmata, and received supernatural favours, the saintly Capuchin friar, Padre Pio, was restricted by the Holy See for about ten years from saying Mass publicly or seeing the people. He submitted in obedience but wept, not on the restriction placed on himself — an isolated life would be easier for him as a contemplative religious — but for all the graces that would be lost to all the people. Padre Pio has since been canonized by Pope John Paul II in 2002. And so, in the cases of Padre Pio and Sr. Faustina, for example, what would many good people have surmised for years but that Rome must be right and that Padre Pio and Sr. Faustina were false witnesses!"

In fact, it was eight years before the apparitions in Lourdes were acknowledged and it took thirteen years before the apparitions in Fatima were approved — and many graces were lost in the interval. Indeed, it is most likely that many authentic apparitions have been wrongly condemned by certain Church officials. But what a responsibility to carry on one's shoulders!

This book is largely about the private revelations of Our Lady in Fatima and those of Berthe Petit of Belgium (1870-1943). Like so many cardinals, bishops and the laity in her era, so impressed was I with her life and messages from Our Lord, that on August 1, 1994, I visited the little village of Louvignies in Belgium and the beautiful and historic tomb where she lies buried in the vault of the family of the Countess de Villegas de Ste. Pierre. More recently, on Monday April 17, 2006 of Holy Week, I returned to Louvignies to place a copy of this book in her vault. Few people in today's Belgium know much about her but the magnificence of her tomb with its numerous marble plaques in tribute to her bespeaks the reverence and respect with which she was held (see pages 7, 8 and 9).

It was Paul who once said: "I am not ashamed of the Gospel" (Romans 1:16). In like manner, this author is not ashamed of authentic private revelations, particularly those officially approved by the Church. Their messages are extremely important for the world and for our salvation.

The vault where Berthe Petit lies buried

The tomb of Berthe Petit beneath the altar

The plaque reads: "Here lies Mlle Berthe Petit, the apostle of the devotion to the Sorrowful and Immaculate Heart of Mary. Born in Einheim on 23 January, 1870 and died in the Lord in Brussels on 26 March, 1943. R.I.P.

Chapter

2

The Sorrowful Heart of Mary

It is recorded in Genesis that a companion was given to Adam. He called her Eve, which meant "mother of the living" (Genesis 3:20). But through her, sin entered the world and she who was the mother of the living became the mother of death. When Eve and then Adam were seduced by the ancient serpent Satan, they were expelled from the Garden of Eden and in Genesis 3:15 it is recorded that God rebuked Satan with words to the effect that a second Eve and a second Adam will crush his head: "Because you have done this, I will put enmity between you and the woman; between your seed and her seed. She will crush your head and you will strike at her heel."

The first Adam and the first Eve were immaculate at birth in that they were born sinless, and so, the second Adam and the second Eve were also born sinless but unlike the first Adam and the first Eve, they remained sinless throughout their life's journey on Earth (Jesus, of course, was incapable of sinning). When in the fullness of time the Archangel Gabriel brought the good news to Mary that she was chosen to be the mother of the Messiah, after seeking an explanation, she accepted the invitation. It was her first recorded "yes" to God and indeed her whole life on Earth has been a perpetual "yes" to Him. With her "yes," it is written that she immediately conceived the God-man, the second Adam, and became the Womb of God. This second Eve restored life to the world through her Son and is truly the everlasting mother of the living. But to be the Womb of God she first had to be the "Immaculate Conception." She was the only exception to the universal law in anticipation of being the God-bearer, the Theotokos.

She became the Mother of God. It was the first Marian dogma. When she gave birth to the Prince of Peace, she became the Queen of Peace. When He bequeathed her to John before He died, she then became the Mother of Mankind. It was the King of all Nations on a hill called Calvary and the Mother of all Nations by His side. Peace was restored between God and man. It was the Man of Sorrows and the Woman of Sorrows. It was the Redeemer and His companion the co-redemptrix. But to be the co-redemptrix being immaculate was not enough. Redemption had to come from suffering, and so, the title co-redemptrix is intimately linked with the title *Sorrowful and Immaculate Heart of Mary.*

On that joyous day when He was born, she wrapped His tiny body in swaddling clothes and placed Him in His crib (Luke 2:12). But on that Friday at the foot of the Cross, thirty three years later, she received His body, tattered and torn and swaddled with blood as He took upon Himself the sins of the world. It was not a pretty sight — but neither is sin in the eyes of God!

Now, the second Adam could have entered into time as a young adult as did the first Adam, but He chose to come as a babe in the womb of a woman. And so, God created His own mother through the incarnation of the Second Person of the Holy Trinity. It may also be said that God so loved the world that He made one of us His mother. She was mother and "companion" of the second Adam, not, as is often written, from the crib to the Cross, but more accurately, from the womb to the tomb. But while she was indeed the "companion" of the Redeemer, cooperating in His act of redemption, she was certainly not co-equal with Him: "I am the handmaid of the Lord," she said (Luke 1:38). This is so unlike the words of the famous hymn of St. Thomas Aquinas, the *Tantum Ergo*:

"Glory to God the Father.
Praise to His co-equal Son."

Forty days after she gave birth to the Prince of Peace, as was the custom, she carried her infant, her only and first-born, to the temple on that day when the holy Simeon prophesied: "This child is destined to be a sign that will be opposed — and a sword shall pierce thine own soul" (Luke 2:35). This was the first warning given to the sorrowful mother of the Suffering Servant of Yahweh, as declared by Pope Paul VI (MC 7), alluding to Isaiah 53. Redemption had to come from suffering, and so, the second Adam and the second Eve were the Sufferer and the Co-sufferer respectively. Redemption came from the passion of the Redeemer and the compassion and co-passion of the Co-redemptrix.

Towards the very end of His journey into time, a journey which He chose so that we would enjoy His company in eternity, and approaching the end of the suffering and ridicule which He endured by His own free will and in obedience to His Father, from His parched tongue and palate, he was able to utter His last will and testament: "Woman (referring to her as the woman of Genesis 3:15), behold your son," and to John, who represented mankind: "Son, behold your mother" (John 19:25-27). He then shouted with a surprisingly loud cry: "It is finished," and bowed his head (John 19:30). And so, redemption which began in Nazareth at the Annunciation was "finished" on Calvary. His mission, or more accurately *Their* mission, was accomplished. It was a mission for the salvation of mankind wherein all things were made new. It was indeed the greatest love story ever told in creation history. It was a man who gave up His life for his friends. Greater love has no man.

There were those compassionate apostles and disciples, who thought that the mother should not witness the Way of the Cross and the Crucifixion, but she insisted that she wanted to be with her Son. And so, when all else fled (except John), she was there at the foot of the Cross. *Stabat mater.* Indeed, if she had not chosen to witness and participate in the Passion of her Son, she could never be called the co-redemptrix. Moreover, it was she who provided Him with the instrument for redemption and suffering — His body. It was a totally Marian body. No human father was involved. His DNA was totally Marian!

Indeed, words could never fully describe in any adequate measure the suffering and anguish of the mother on that day. Perhaps it can be appreciated somewhat if every mother were to contemplate her own son on the cross in place of the Son of Mary. Yet if there were a thousand such mothers standing at the feet of a thousand crosses bearing their thousand crucified sons, the sum total of their anguish could not in any way measure the pain, sorrow and suffering of that *Mother of Sorrows* on that hill on that Friday that some men call "Good." She too was being co-crucified.

As Rev. Cyril Papali in his book, *Mother of God, Mary in Scripture and Tradition*, wrote: "Hers is the most spiritual and the most pure, the most selfless, the most intense and incomprehensible suffering ever known. One solitary creature suffering *with* God and *for* God, suffering *for* all mankind and *from* them — that is the price for becoming Co-redemptrix. That is the meaning of being the second Eve.

St. Bernard of Clairvaux (1090-1153) also recognized the rationale for and intensity of her suffering when he wrote: "One man and one woman harmed us grievously. Thanks to God, all things are restored by one man and one woman, and that with interest! It is true that Christ would have been adequate since all our sufficiency is from Him, but it was not good for us that it should be a man alone. It was more appropriate that both sexes should take part in our reparation since both had wrought our ruin. But her cooperation means much more than this. It implies the true dependence of the whole work of redemption on her free will because God Himself willed it to be conditioned by her consent. In that sense redemption in its entirety is a cooperative work also and for that reason alone she deserves to be called Co-redemptrix."

In his classic book *The Glories of Mary*, St. Alphonsus de Liguori (1696-1787), the Founder of the Redemptorists and Doctor of the Church, in speaking of the Blessed Virgin, wrote: "The Blessed Virgin is so great and sublime that the more she is praised the more there remains to praise; so much so, says an ancient writer, that if all the tongues of men were put together, and even if each of their members were changed into a tongue, they would not suffice to praise her as much as she deserves."

In his chapters on *"The Dolours of Mary,"* he wrote: "As Jesus is called the King of Sorrows and the King of Martyrs because He suffered during His life more than all of the martyrs, so also is Mary with reason called the Queen of Martyrs, having merited this title by suffering the most cruel martyrdom possible after that of her Son. It is an undoubted opinion that suffering sufficient to cause death is martyrdom even though death does not ensue from it. 'Mary was a martyr,' says Saint Bernard, 'not by the sword of the executioner but by bitter sorrow of heart.' If her body was not wounded by the hand of the executioner, her blessed heart was transfixed by a sword of grief at the Passion of her Son; a grief which was sufficient to have caused her death, not once but a thousand times."

St. Alphonsus also quoted St. Bonaventure, who remarked that "those wounds which were scattered over the Body of Our Lord were all united in the single heart of Mary. To understand the greatness of Mary's grief at the death of her Son, we must understand the greatness of the love she bore for Him. But who can ever measure that love? Since there has never been in the world a love like unto Mary's love, how can any sorrow be found like unto Mary's sorrow? It is all prophesied soon after the birth of her Son when Simeon warned: 'This child is destined to be a sign that will be opposed — and thy own soul a sword shall pierce' " (Luke 2:35).

Now, the heart is the word which has been used most

often in the Bible. In fact, it occurs about 700 times, even more than the word "God" or "Lord." The first time it is mentioned is in Genesis 6:5-6: "The Lord saw that the wickedness of man was great on the earth... It grieved him to his heart." But just as the physical heart, that wondrous and untiring organ, which incessantly beats during life, the Heart of Jesus as an object of devotion is a reflection of His untiring love for man. It is His physical Heart which during His mortal life did beat in His breast and still beats in His glorified Body in Heaven. Indeed, God *is* Love and His Heart is the symbol of that Love!

St. Bridget of Sweden (1303-1373) learned from Jesus Himself about the loving identity and oneness of the two Hearts. In fact, in the fourteenth century it was said that she was told by Jesus: "The heart of My mother was like Mine. Therefore, I confirm that we worked together for the salvation of mankind. I, by the sufferings endured in My Body, she by the sorrows and by the love in her heart." Indeed, St. John Eudes (1601-1680), who wrote many books on the Heart of Jesus and Mary, never used the plural as he preached that "the Heart of Jesus and Mary *is* one."

However, the great apostle of the devotion to the Sacred Heart was St. Margaret Mary Alacoque. She received this message from Our Lord on December 27, 1673: "My divine Heart is so inflamed with love for men, and for you in particular, that It is unable any longer to contain within Itself the flames of Its burning love. It needs to spread them abroad through you and so manifest Itself to them in order to enrich them with the precious treasures which this Heart contains, graces of holiness and salvation, which are necessary to withdraw them from the abyss of perdition. I have chosen you, in spite of your unworthiness and lack of knowledge, for the accomplishment of this great design so that it may better appear that it has been done by Myself."

In June 1675, Jesus appeared again to St. Margaret in all His splendor in what is called "The Great Revelation": "Behold this Heart," He said, "which has so much love for men that It spared nothing, even to exhausting and consuming Itself in order to give them testimony of Its love. If only they would give Me some return for My love, I would think but little of all that I have done for them and would wish, were it possible, to suffer still more. But in return I mostly received only ingratitude, through the irreverence and sacrileges, through the coldness and scorn that they have for Me in the Sacrament of Love. But what gives Me more sorrow is that there are hearts consecrated to Me who treat Me thus. Do you at least console Me by making up for the ingratitude as far as you can… I will reign through My heart despite Satan and his agents, in spite of all those who oppose this devotion."

Now what is described as the first of Mary's apparitions in modern times took place in 1830 when she, who herself had received an apparition from the Archangel Gabriel in Nazareth, appeared to St. Catherine Labouré in the Convent of the Sisters of Charity in the Rue du Bac in Paris. In November of that year she showed the nun in a vision a medallion which was called at that time the Medal of the Immaculate Conception. On one side of that medallion Catherine was shown a large M surmounted by a Cross and beneath it were two Hearts, one with a crown of thorns and the other pierced by a sword. Those two Hearts were the symbols of Their love while the crown of thorns (of Jesus) and the sword (of Simeon) represented Their sorrows and suffering which were necessary for redemption. That 1830 vision in the Rue du Bac with its medallion was the first symbolic depiction of the Redeemer and the Co-redemptrix.

Then in 1846, the Woman of Sorrows appeared in La Salette, France on September 19, at that time the eve of the feast of the Seven Sorrows of Our Lady, weeping copiously. As described by the chosen visionary of that event, Melanie Calvat: "The Holy Virgin was crying nearly the whole time that she was speaking to me. Her tears flowed gently, one by one, down to her knees, then like sparks of light they disappeared. These tears of our sweet mother, far from lessening her air of majesty of a queen, seemed on the contrary to embellish her, to make her more beautiful, more powerful, more filled with love, more maternal, more ravishing. Is it possible to see a mother cry, and such a mother, without doing anything possible to comfort her and change her grief into joy?"

Mel Gibson's *The Passion of the Christ* is indisputably the best film portrayal ever of the suffering of Christ, but even that portrayal did not approximate the true extent of the suffering that He actually endured on that Friday. Both Gibson's movie and my book *The Passion of the Christ and His Mother* were based on the revelations of the 19th century nun and mystic Anne Catherine Emmerich, who was beatified by Pope John Paul II in Rome on October 3, 2004. However, I did try in my book to depict in more graphic detail the intense co-suffering of the mother moreso than the film did and as St. Anne Catherine saw it in her visions.

Chapter

3

World War I and Berthe Petit

What are little known worldwide are the private revelations of Our Lord which were made public through the respected and very holy Belgium mystic and stigmatist, Berthe Petit, a Franciscan Tertiary (1870-1943). She enjoyed the highest respect of cardinals, bishops, theologians and other members of the Church hierarchy in her time. She was, as it were, a child of the era of the two world wars. The prelude to World War I was the Franco-Prussian War of 1870. It was in that year she was born. That war was followed by World War I in 1914, which, in turn, led to World War II in 1939. Mlle Petit died in 1943 toward the end of World War II.

While attending midnight Mass in 1909, she saw the wounded Heart of Jesus and closely adherent to it was the Heart of Mary pierced with a sword. Then she heard these words: "Cause My mother's Heart transfixed by the sorrows that rent Mine to be loved." Then on February 7, 1910, she was shown the Hearts of Jesus and Mary interpenetrating each other and hovering over the Hearts was a Dove (See page 39). Jesus then said: "You must think of My mother's Heart as you think of Mine; live in this Heart as you seek to live in Mine; give yourself to this Heart as you give yourself to Mine. You must spread the love of this Heart so wholly united to Mine." A few days later her mission was revealed to her. It was to obtain the consecration of the whole world to the *Sorrowful and Immaculate Heart of Mary*.

For many years this holy Franciscan Tertiary, while leading a life of hidden suffering in the world, a voluntary victim for the expiation of sin, received repeated revelations from Our Lord of His desire that the **whole world** should be publicly consecrated to the *Sorrowful and Immaculate Heart*. During Mass, she once saw the divine face under a crown of thorns in a great glory of light at the moment of the elevation of the Host. Our Lord then repeated: "The world must be dedicated to the *Sorrowful and Immaculate Heart* of My mother as it is dedicated to Mine. Fear nothing, no matter what suffering and obstacles you may meet. Think only of fulfilling My will."

On Easter Sunday, 1910, while in Rome, Berthe again saw the Hearts of Jesus and Mary fused with each other under the wing of a dove. This time she heard: "What I desire derives from what I did on Calvary. In giving John to My mother for her son, I confided the whole world to her *Sorrowful and Immaculate Heart*." Our Lord then bade her to make a drawing of the vision of the two Hearts(see page 39), adding: "I will guide your hand." A few months later, she received a further communication from Jesus: "I desire that the picture for which I guided your hand should be widely diffused as well as the invocation '*Sorrowful and Immaculate Heart of Mary, pray for us*.'"

On September 8, 1910, soon after receiving Holy Communion, Our Lord said to her: "The Heart of My mother has a right to be called *Sorrowful* and I wish this title to be placed *before* that of *Immaculate* because she has won it herself. The Church has defined in the case of My mother what I Myself had ordained — her Immaculate Conception. This right which My mother has to a title of justice is now, according to My express wish, to be known and universally accepted. She has earned it by her identification with My sorrows, by her sufferings, by her sacrifices and by her immolation on Calvary, endured in perfect correspondence with My grace for the salvation of mankind. In her co-redemption lies the nobility of My mother and for this reason I ask for the invocation which I have demanded be approved and spread throughout the whole Church. It has already obtained many graces; it will obtain yet more when the Church will be exalted and the world renewed through its consecration to the *Sorrowful and Immaculate Heart of My mother.*"

Nine days later, on September 17, 1910, the mother herself appeared to Berthe and revealed in a symbolic way the bodily martyrdom that she suffered at the foot of the Cross. Berthe saw her brow wounded and bleeding and her hands and heart pierced. She then said: "Now you can understand the sorrows which my Heart endured and the sufferings of my whole being for the salvation of the world." Then at a Holy Hour devotion during the night of March 24-25, 1912, the eve of the feast of the Annunciation, the Blessed Virgin spoke again to Berthe of her **Sorrowful Heart**: "I am called the Immaculate Conception. With you, I call myself the *Mother of the Sorrowful Heart*. This title *that my Son wants* is the dearest to me of all my titles and it is through it that shall be granted and spread everywhere, graces of mercy, spiritual renewal and salvation."

July 12, 1912 marked the beginning of a different phase in the mystical experiences of Berthe Petit. Until that time her heavenly communications dealt solely with religious matters but on that day she received the first of several revelations concerning political events. They were similar to some of the messages of a political nature which were given by the Blessed Virgin Mary to St. Catherine Labouré in 1830, by the Virgin of La Salette to Melanie Calvat and Maximin Giraud in 1846 when she wept copiously, and, as we shall see later, to Ida Peerdeman in Amsterdam in 1945–1984.

On that day, July 12, 1912, Jesus told Berthe that the heir to the Catholic empire of Austria-Hungary would be assassinated: "A double murder will strike down the successor of the aged sovereign, so loyal to the faith." He was referring to Archduke Franz Josef I (1830-1916), who was 82 years old at the time. Jesus added: "It will be the *first* of those events (World Wars) full of sorrows, but from whence I shall still bring forth good and which will precede the chastisement."

This prophecy was fulfilled a little less than two years later on June 28, 1914 when Archduke Franz Ferdinand and his wife Sophia, the Duchess of Hohenburg, were assassinated by 19 year old Gavrilo Princip, a Serbian nationalist. The following day, June 29, Jesus said to Berthe: "Now begins the ascending curve of preliminary events, which will lead to the great manifestation of My justice." Indeed, that "preliminary event" in Sarajevo led to World War I which started about five weeks later on August 4, 1914 when Germany invaded Belgium and violated its neutrality which was guaranteed by Britain, Germany and France in the treaty of 1839. However, Kaiser Wilhelm II dismissed the treaty as a mere "piece of paper." At that time Belgium was a very Catholic country and the Catholic political party was in control. By midnight Great Britain and Germany were at war. That war eventually led to World War II, which may possibly culminate in a World War III in this nuclear age and with the annihilation of several nations.

According to Mlle Petit, when the Germans entered Brussels, just as He harshly criticized the Pharisees, as recorded in the Gospels, Jesus had harsh words to say about the German invaders: "The proud race and its ambitious ruler (Kaiser Wilhelm II) will be chastised on the very soil (Belgium) of their unjust conquest... The worst calamities which I predicted are unleashed. The time has now arrived when I wish mankind to turn to the *Sorrowful and Immaculate Heart of My mother*. Let this prayer be uttered by every soul: '*Sorrowful and Immaculate Heart of Mary, pray for us*' so that it may spread as a refreshing and purifying balm of reparation that will appease My anger. This devotion to the *Sorrowful and Immaculate Heart of My mother* will restore faith and hope to broken hearts and to ruined families. It will help to repair the destruction. It will sweeten sorrow. It will be a new strength for My Church, bringing souls, not only to confidence in My Heart, but also to abandonment to the *Sorrowful Heart of My mother*."

Pope Pius X died on August 10, 1914 soon after World War I began and he was succeeded by Giacomo della Chiesa, who chose the name Pope Benedict XV (1914-1922). As Sir Nicholas Cheetham commented in his *History of the Popes:* "How ought the Holy See to react to a murderous conflict in which Catholic Austria–Hungary and partly-Catholic Germany stood initially opposed to an alliance of Catholic, but officially irreligious France, with Orthodox Russia and Protestant Great Britain?" This indeed was the problem facing Pope Benedict, shortly to be complicated by Italy's entry into the war. In his first statement on September 8, 1914, the feast of the Nativity of the Blessed Virgin Mary, he mourned the bloodshed and pleaded for a quick end to the war just begun. He also denounced the war as a crime against religion, humanity and civilization, perpetrated as it was by Catholic countries.

Then, in his first encyclical *Ad Beatissimi Apostolorum*, issued on November 1, 1914, Pope Benedict criticized the warring Christian peoples: "Who could realize," he wrote, "that they are the children of the same Father in Heaven?" He then closed with a call for a prayer to Christ and the Blessed Virgin Mary, "who bore the Prince of Peace." Then the following year, on May 31, 1915, eight days after Italy entered the war, he sent a letter to the Dean of the Sacred College, Cardinal Venutelli, which concluded with the following recommendation addressed to all the bishops of the world: "Let us send up our prayers, more than ever ardent and frequent, to Him in whose Hands lie the destinies of all peoples, and let us appeal with confidence to the *Sorrowful and Immaculate Heart of Mary* (*quoting the invocation requested by Berthe Petit*), the most gentle Mother of Jesus and ours, that by her powerful intercession she will obtain from her divine Son the speedy end of the war and the return of peace and tranquility."

Now, following Belgium's invasion and occupation, Berthe Petit spent the years of World War I in neutral Switzerland where she was frequently told in advance of the calamities that would befall the Allies. The two Cardinals who cooperated most with her were Cardinal Desiré Mercier, Primate of Belgium, and Cardinal Francis Alphonsus Bourne, the Primate of England and Archbishop of Canterbury. Cardinal Bourne (1861-1935) became acclaimed for his patriotic speeches during the war and Cardinal Mercier (1851-1926) became the spokesman of Belgian opposition to the German occupation for which the Germans placed him under house arrest.

He was Berthe's spiritual director for several years, was deeply impressed by her heavenly communications, and energetically promoted the devotion to the *Sorrowful and Immaculate Heart of Mary* in Belgium. In fact, he had also approached the predecessor of Pope Benedict XV, Pope Pius X (1903–1914), and attempted to win his approval for the worldwide devotion. Seventeen petitions were made to the Pope, however, sadly to say, the Pope did not find it appropriate to promote a new worldwide devotion at that time, but it was certainly never condemned on doctrinal grounds. However, like Pius X, Pope Benedict XV also did not judge the time opportune for a worldwide devotion.

In February, 1915, Our Lord said to Berthe: "It is through the *Sorrowful and Immaculate Heart* of My mother that I will triumph, because having cooperated in the redemption of souls, this Heart has the right to share a similar cooperation in the manifestations of My justice and of My love. My mother is noble in everything but she is especially so in her wounded heart, transfixed by the wound of Mine."

Berthe in the interim remained quietly patient in Switzerland awaiting God's good pleasure and continued to receive heavenly communications. Our Lady later showed her in a vision an untold multitude of every race and colour, sick and suffering, all praying with arms raised to heaven. Some were physically healed, others, touched by grace, fell on their knees. "It seemed a *regeneration* of the whole world," said Berthe. (I thought to myself that what Berthe saw in that vision was probably the fruit yet to come from the prayer of the "Lady of All Nations" given to Ida Peerdeman in 1951 in Amsterdam (See Chapter 7): "Lord Jesus Christ, Son of the Father, send now Your Spirit over the earth. Let the Holy Spirit live in the hearts of all nations so that they may be preserved from *degeneration*, disasters and war...").

Meanwhile, as the war continued, on March 7, 1916 Cardinal Mercier announced that during the Good Friday ceremonies he would dedicate his diocese and his beloved country Belgium to the *Sorrowful and Immaculate Heart of Mary,* and in England Cardinal Bourne continued to rally the faithful towards this devotion. In a pastoral letter of September 3, 1916, he wrote: "Nowhere in Christendom should honour be paid more readily to the *Sorrowful and Immaculate Heart of Mary* than here in England. In the days of united faith (that is, before the Reformation), her purity and her sorrows were ever held in loving veneration. Throughout the realm, Our Blessed Lady, God's mother, were terms and titles dear to every English heart. England was, in very truth, Our Lady's dowry. It is therefore not with the idea of introducing any new devotion, but rather in order to give fresh meaning and greater force to thoughts long cherished by us all and deep-rooted in the history of our race that we desire to consecrate with renewed effort the prayer, which the special circumstances of the moment so urgently demand, to the *Sorrowful and Immaculate Heart of Mary*...

"For these reasons, we desire and enjoin that in all the churches and public chapels of our diocese, Friday, September 15, the feast of the Seven Sorrows of Our Blessed Lady, or on the following Sunday, during Benediction of the Blessed Sacrament, the *Stabat Mater* be sung, to be followed by the recitation of three Hail Marys and the invocation (repeated after each Hail Mary) '*Sorrowful and Immaculate Heart of Mary, pray for us*,' in order that, by this public homage, all our dioceses, and, insofar in us lies, our whole country and empire may be solemnly consecrated and dedicated to Our Blessed Lady under this special title."

That day, September 15, 1916, the feast of Our Lady of Sorrows, was a very historic day. It was the first taste of victory by the British in the costly and long Battle of the Somme. As a reporter wrote at that time, "they laughed even while blood was streaming down their faces." These were the infantrymen who went into battle on the Somme with a new weapon, conceived and built in strictest secrecy under the code name "Tank." Within two hours the British and Canadians had taken more than 2,000 prisoners. These motor monsters, as the men called them, transformed the whole character of the war.

In fact, each time public devotions were performed in England, the British armies swept forward to unexpected victories so much so that Marshal Ferdinand Foch, the Commander in Chief of the Allied forces in France, observed in his "*Memoires*" that, strangely enough, the English seemed scarcely aware of how those successes could have come about. "I will never repeat it too often," he wrote, "that the English fought in a most extraordinary way. They won victory upon victory. At the beginning of October they had broken the formidable Hindenburg line at its strongest point. But still more wonderful, these victories were won almost unknown to themselves." Among those notable successes of the war by the Allies was the capture of the village of Passchendaele by the Canadians ending the third battle of Ypres and the enemy then lost all hope of piercing the line to Calais. There was also the success of the Allies in driving back the Germans on the Marne, relieving the threat to Paris.

On August 15, 1917, the feast of the Assumption of the Blessed Virgin Mary, Cardinal Bourne once more consecrated England to the *Sorrowful Heart of Mary* (This was repeated solemnly on Christmas day). On August 22, 1917, the feast of the Queenship of Mary, Our Lord sent the following message through Berthe Petit to Cardinal Bourne: "I ask My apostle Francis to exert an ever increasing activity in favour of the *Sorrowful and Immaculate Heart of My mother* ... Let him hasten what he calls his 'first step' so that a still more solemn consecration may be timed for the feast of the Sorrows of My mother — that great feast of her Heart as Co-redemptrix. When the nation (England) of my apostle Francis will be entirely dedicated to this Heart he will see that he has not listened to My word in vain, for My providential intervention is reserved for all the people consecrated to the *Sorrowful and Immaculate Heart of My mother*. I wish thus to show the power of this Heart which is linked in everything with My own."

When the tide of battle turned against the Allies in the dreadful spring of 1918, Jesus explained to Berthe: "It is a necessary trial for after My protection had helped them to conquer, they attributed the glory to their own prowess. Reverses are now showing these soldiers how human means alone are powerless to repel the surge of invasion."

However, by mid-October 1918, the Germans were all but finished and desertions were skyrocketing. People had had enough. Governments fell and chaos prevailed over central Europe. Then on October 17, 1918, Our Lord told Berthe: "Were it not for My intervention, obtained by My apostle Francis through recourse to the *Sorrowful and Immaculate Heart of My mother,* the victory would have belonged to those who strained every nerve during so many years to prepare and organize a great war for the attainment of their own ambitions .... Material force would have overborne justice and right and this more especially so for your own country (Belgium). For why should I come to the help of a people in France intent on persecuting My Church. That is why trials will continue until the day when, humbly acknowledging her errors, this nation will render Me My rights and give full liberty to My Church."

During that month Our Lord also warned Berthe: "The world is hanging on the edge of utter cataclysm. My justice cannot preside over the machination of those who work in their own interests to forward a peace totally unworthy of the name, and which can never be genuine except through My intervention." He was referring to the notorious Versailles Peace Treaty in Paris at the end of World War I.

Three weeks later, after the most bloody conflict among the nations, and after ten million people had died and many more maimed and displaced, the greatest global war in known history at that time ended abruptly and gloriously in favour of the British. It was at eleven a.m. on the eleventh day of the eleventh month of 1918 when the Armistice took place. It was on the feast of St. Martin of Tours, the patron saint of soldiers! On May 24, 1919, the Archbishop of Westminster again consecrated his country to the *Sorrowful and Immaculate Heart of Mary* in thanksgiving for the great victory in what was thought to be "the war to end all wars."

In July, 1919, eight months after the Armistice, Our Lord spoke as follows to Berthe: "Internal strife is more rampant than ever in your country. It is being fanned by the evil seed sown by the invader. It is fed by egoism, pride and jealousy — malevolent germs which can only generate moral ruin... Time will prove that a peace established without Me and without him who speaks in My name (referring to Pope Benedict XV) has no stability. The nation (Germany) which is considered to be vanquished but whose forces are only momentarily diminished, will remain a menace for your country and likewise for France. Confusion and terror will steadily spread through every nation. Because this peace is not Mine, wars will be rekindled on every side — civil war and racial war. What would have been so noble, so true, so beautiful, so lasting in its fulfillment is consequently delayed. Humanity is advancing towards a frightful scourge which will divide the nations more and more. It will reduce human schemes to nothingness. It will break the pride of the powers that be. It will show that nothing subsists without Me and that I remain the sole Master of the destinies of nations."

"A peace totally unworthy of the name," said Our Lord to Berthe. Let us research the history of that rebuke. Now, Pope

Benedict XV had adopted a rigidly neutral position between the belligerents and while denouncing the war as a crime against religion, humanity and civilization, he had blamed both sides equally for allowing it to happen and to continue. However, neither side appreciated his attitude nor responded to his exhortations. In fact, it later transpired that one of Italy's conditions for entering the war in 1915 with the Allies was the exclusion of the Holy See from any eventual peace conference.

After his suggestion of a general Christmas truce in 1914 was totally ignored by the Allies, on August 1, 1917, Benedict XV issued a 7-point peace plan to each of the belligerent nations. Ignored by most powers, only Austria-Hungary regarded it with any degree of seriousness. However, the Pope strove continually and imperturbably for a negotiated peace as opposed to a dictated one, and being barred from the Palace Peace Conference which began in January 1919 in Paris, caused him to stigmatize the Treaty of Versailles (not unfairly) as a "consecration of hatred" and a "perpetuation of war."

Germany had refused to acknowledge any sole guilt and responsibility for the war and the German people, having agreed to set about forming a democratic republican government, felt that they were entitled to a just peace. However, when the terms of the Versailles Treaty, laid down by the Allies without negotiation with Germany, were published in Berlin on May 7, 1919, they came as a staggering blow to the German people. Germany was made to pay "reparations" far beyond her power of payment and in contravention of the plain understandings upon which she had surrendered. She was put in a position of economic serfdom.

Angry mass meetings were then organized throughout

the country to protest against the treaty and to demand that Germany refuse to sign it. Indeed, the treaty was branded as "unreasonable and unbearable" and intolerable for any nation, so much so that Phillipp Scheidemann, who had become the first Chancellor of the Weimar Assembly, exclaimed: "May the hand wither that signs this treaty!" In fact, Field Marshall von Hindenburg, President of Germany, came to the conclusion that he could not help feeling that it was better to perish honourably than accept a disgraceful peace.

However, the Treaty of Versailles was eventually signed in the Hall of Mirrors in the Palace of Versailles on June 28, 1919 with objections from the German government, protesting that they did so "under the threat of force." On that day Germany became a house divided. When he read the Peace Treaty, Marshall Ferdinand Foch, the Commander in Chief of the Allied Forces in France, burst out: "This is not peace! This is an armistice for twenty years." Indeed, twenty years and sixty-seven days later, once more militant Germany was at war with Great Britain and France. As Our Lord had previously said to Berthe Petit: "Time will prove that a peace established without Me and without him who speaks in My name has no stability."

Yet another critic of the Versailles Peace Treaty was Winston Churchill. In his book *The Second World War*, he began this *magnum opus* with these words: "The economic clauses of the Treaty were malignant and silly to an extent that made them obviously futile. Germany was condemned to pay reparations on a fabulous scale. The triumphant Allies continued to assert that they would squeeze Germany 'till the pips squeaked' and that Germany should be made to pay 'to the uttermost farthing.'

All this had a potent bearing on the prosperity of the world and the mood of the German race. History will characterise all these transactions as insane. They helped to breed both the martial curse and the economic blizzard. All this was a sad story of complicated idiocy in the making of which much toil and virtue was consumed. Thereafter mighty forces were adrift, the void was open, and into that void, after a pause, there stood a maniac of ferocious genius, the repository and expression of the most virulent hatreds that have ever corroded the human breast — Corporal Hitler."

Now, a picture of Our Lady, referred later as Our Lady of Ollignies, is of mysterious origin. It was discovered in Ollignies in Belgium under precarious circumstances in 1918 in the convent of the Bernadine nuns by whom Berthe Petit had been educated. After the withdrawal of the German troops from Belgium, consequent on the closure of the war, one of the Sisters was asked to put the cellar in order. Among the various items she found was a piece of cardboard wrapped in an old newspaper with pornographic pictures, which she tore off to be burnt along with other rubbish. However, to her astonishment she found underneath the cardboard, a beautiful picture of Our Lady. This was reported to the Mother Superior and the whole community then felt that their safety during the war was probably due to the special protection of Our Lady manifested by that picture within the precincts of the convent. However, in spite of thorough investigations they were unable to trace its origin.

When it was shown to Berthe Petit in 1919 on returning from Switzerland after the war, she at once recognized it as a picture of the two-fold symbols of the *Sorrowful and*

Immaculate Heart of Mary. The image in the picture represented the Mother of God, holding in her left hand a lily, the symbol of her immaculate purity, that gratuitous gift of her divine Son, and the finger of her right hand pointed to her Sorrowful Heart surmounted by flames and pierced with a sword. Soon it became widely known and sought after all over Belgium (see page 37).

The painting of the Sorrowful and Immaculate Heart of Mary found in the convent in Ollignies

Berthe Petit

Berthe Petit's vision of the two Hearts

Chapter

4

The Ultimate Message of Fatima

World War I was still raging when on May 5, 1917, in a letter to his Secretary of State, Cardinal Pietro Gasparri, Pope Benedict XV wrote: "Our earnestly pleading voice, invoking the end of this vast conflict, the suicide of civilized Europe, was then and has remained ever since unheard. Since all graces which the Author of all good deigns to grant to the poor children of Adam, by a loving design of His Divine Providence, are dispensed through the hands of the Most Holy Virgin, we wish that the petition of her most afflicted children, more than ever in this terrible hour, may turn with lively confidence to the august *Mother of God.*"

He then directed that the invocation, "Queen of Peace, pray for us," be added permanently to the Litany of Loreto and made his ultimate appeal to her: "To Mary, who is the *Mother of Mercy* and omnipotent by grace, let this loving and devout appeal go up from every corner of the earth from noble temples and tiniest chapels, from royal palaces and mansions of the rich as from the poorest hut, from every place where a faithful soul finds shelter from blood-drenched plains and seas. Let it bear to her the anguished cry of mothers and wives, the wailing of innocent little ones, the sighs of every generous heart; let her most tender and benign solicitude be moved and the peace we ask for be obtained for our agitated world."

Now, Portugal, since its very foundation, was called "*La Terra de Santa Maria*" and in 1646, two hundred years before Our Lady appeared in Lourdes, King Dom John IV of Portugal and the entire nation swore fidelity to Mary under the title of "The Immaculate Conception." Since that year, the Mother of God was proclaimed Queen and Patroness of Portugal. For that reason, the Portuguese monarchs never wore a crown. It has been reserved exclusively for the immaculate Virgin.

Eight days after the appeal of Pope Benedict XV, on Sunday May 13, 1917, the Blessed Virgin responded to his prayers and those of the rest of the Catholic world and appeared to three children, Lucia, Jacinta and Francisco, in a little village called Fatima in Portugal. "I come from Heaven," she said. "I want you to come here on the 13th of each month until October when I will tell you who I am and what I want." In her last words on that day, she stressed the immense crisis which had brought her from Heaven and implored: "Say the Rosary to obtain peace for the world and the end of the war."

The following month on June 13, she showed the children a vision of her Heart encircled by piercing thorns, which obviously represented, not simply her Immaculate Heart, that gratuitous gift from God, but her *Sorrowful and Immaculate Heart*. She then said to Lucia: "God wishes you to remain in the world for some time because He wants you to establish in the world devotion to my *Immaculate Heart* for the Heart of Jesus wants my *Immaculate Heart* to be venerated by His side. I promise salvation to those who embrace it and their souls would be loved by God as the flowers placed by myself adorning His throne."

On July 13, she said to the little seers: "The war (World War I) is going to end soon, but if people will not stop offending God, another more terrible war will begin during the reign of Pius XI (1922-1939). To prevent this, I now come to ask for the consecration of **Russia** to my *Immaculate Heart* and the Communion of Reparation on the five first Saturdays. If my request is granted, Russia will be converted and there will be peace. If not, she will scatter her errors throughout the world, provoking wars and the persecution of the Church. The good would be martyred, the Holy Father will have much to suffer and *various nations will be annihilated.* In the end my *Immaculate Heart* will triumph; the Holy Father will consecrate Russia to me, Russia will be converted and a certain period of peace will be granted to the world."

It is important to recall that Russia at that time was still a very Christian country, mainly Orthodox, and that the Communist revolution did not take place until October of that year. Note that she did not *speak* of her *Sorrowful Heart* in Fatima as will be explained later. Also note that in Fatima she asked for the consecration specifically of **Russia** (not the world) to her *Immaculate Heart.*

The last of the monthly apparitions took place on October 13, 1917. It was on a Friday. Expectations were high as the Blessed Virgin had promised the children during the first apparition on May 13 that in October she would say who she was and would perform a miracle. The Cova da Iria was crowded with 70,000

— 43 —

spectators to witness the promised miracle in October. Needless to say, there were also many skeptics among the multitude. The ground was quite muddy from a heavy downpour of rain that day and there were umbrellas in abundance beneath a canopy of grey, cloudy and rainy skies.

According to Dr. Joseph Garret, Professor of Natural Sciences at Coimbra University of Portugal, as quoted by Francis Johnston in his book *Fatima. The Great Sign:* "It must have been about half past one when there rose up, on the precise spot where the children were, *a column of smoke, a delicate, slender, bluish column* that went straight up to about two metres and then evaporated. The phenomenon lasted for some seconds and was perfectly visible to the eye… It was repeated yet a second and third time. On these three occasions, and especially on the last one, the slender posts stood out distinctly against the *dull grey atmosphere."*

Soon afterwards, the children in Fatima saw the usual flash of light from the east, which always preceded the apparitions of Her Majesty in Portugal. To quote Lucia's own words: "We saw the flash of light and then Our Lady appeared on the holm oak tree. She said: 'I want to tell you that a chapel is to be built here in my honour.' And then, as promised on May 13, she at last disclosed who she was: *"I am the Lady of the Rosary.* Continue to pray the Rosary everyday. The war is going to end and the soldiers will soon return to their homes."

Looking upward, the Queen of the Universe then opened her hands and it seemed to Lucia that a light arose straight up from them to the very zenith of the grey skies. The clouds then parted, the sun appeared in the blue window, and the three children saw a tableau of the Holy Family. As recorded by John Haffert in his book *In Her Own Words*, Lucia herself described the three final visions while the sun whirled and people thought that the world was coming to an end: "First appeared St. Joseph with the Child Jesus blessing the world. Our Lady stood beside her holy spouse, clothed in a white tunic and a blue mantle. Next, Our Lord appeared in His glorified manhood. He too blessed the world as St. Joseph had done. Beside Him was His *Co-redemptrix, Our Lady of Sorrows, to whom He had entrusted the peace of the world.* Finally, Our Lady came under her ancient title of Mt. Carmel. She held the Child Jesus in her arms while holding the scapular down to the world."

The *Diario de Noticias* (The Daily News) in Fatima, which commanded the largest circulation in Portugal at the time, described the miracle of the sun on October 1917: "More than 70,000 people gathered at the place of the apparitions. A wave of devotion seemed to take hold of those many thousands of believers and curious alike. As a great number of people had their umbrellas open, the little one (Lucia) asked the people to shut them. Then an extraordinary thing happened. According to the testimony of thousands present there, the sun appeared like a dull silver plate spinning around in a circular movement as if it were moved by electricity, according to the expression used by knowledgeable people who witnessed the fact. Then thousands of people, swayed by emotion and who knows, even dazzled by the light of the sun that had appeared for the first time that day, fell to the ground weeping and raising their hands, joined instinctively in prayer. On their faces an expression of ecstatic rapture could be observed. Their simple hearts prayed and they wept in the presence of this strange sensation, which for them at the moment was miraculous. According to what we heard, there were people who seemed to see the sun leave its supposed orbit, break through the clouds and descend to the horizon, many crying out in fear that the giant orb would precipitate itself to the earth on top of them, and implored the protection of the Holy Virgin. After ten minutes the sun retreated to its celestial abode. The spectators were rescued, as it were, from apparent *annihilation*."

October 13, 1917 was indeed an unforgettable experience for those 70,000 people. The poet Alonzo Lopez Viera saw the miracle of the sun from his own house. Other distant witnesses of this event absolutely destroyed any theory of mass suggestion or hallucination generated by emotion and expectation as an explanation of what was seen in the sky.

But at that time science knew little about nuclear fission and fusion of atoms. An atom with its central nucleus is the smallest possible piece of an element. However, it was not until 1938 that the German physicist Otto Hahn discovered the new radioactive process: nuclear fission. It is a splitting of the nucleus of an atom with the release of a huge amount of heat energy. This is the principle behind the atom bomb. Nuclear fusion, on the other hand, is the joining together of two atoms of the lightest element, hydrogen, to form helium, which is the second lightest element by atomic weight. An extremely high temperature is needed before hydrogen is affected by this nuclear reaction.

We now know that the sun is a gigantic ball of hydrogen nearly 1 million miles in diameter and in its core there is a furnace of about 15,000,000 degrees C (water boils at 100° C), which continually converts hydrogen into helium by the fusion process. This nuclear fusion reaction in the sun has resulted in continuous explosions over the past five billion years (the estimated age of the sun). It is these continuous nuclear explosions which illuminate the planets and sustain life on Earth.

In fact, the idea of a hydrogen bomb is to produce an extremely rapid conversion of hydrogen into helium, that is, to do exactly what the sun does but to do it quickly. This is achieved by enclosing a device causing an extremely high temperature in the bomb. This scale of temperature occurs during enclosure of a neutron or plutonium bomb. It is about 150,000,000°, which is about 10 times greater than the temperature at the centre or core of the sun. In other words, the sun, our nearest star, is a gigantic nuclear reactor, a continuously-exploding hydrogen bomb. The miracle of the sun on October 13, 1917, its apparent falling to Earth and its subsequent return to its celestial position at the command of the Queen of Portugal now assumes an apocalyptic significance!

Francisco died from the influenza epidemic on April 4, 1919 and Jacinta died on Friday February 16, 1920. Shortly before going to the hospital in Lisbon, Jacinta said to Lucia: "It will not be long now before I go to Heaven. You will remain here to announce that God wishes devotion to the *Immaculate Heart* to be established in the world, and that the Heart of Jesus wishes the Heart of Mary to be venerated at His side. Let them ask for peace through the *Immaculate Heart* of Mary for **God has entrusted the peace of the world to her.**"

Now, on December 10, 1925, eight years after the last apparition in Fatima, Her Majesty appeared to Sr. Lucia when she was a postulant in the Dorothean (named after St. Dorothy) Convent in Pontevedra, Spain, and by her side, elevated on a luminous cloud, was the Child Jesus. The Blessed Virgin held her Heart encircled by sharp thorns. The Child Jesus spoke first: "Have compassion on the Heart of your Most Holy Mother, covered with thorns, with which ungrateful men pierce it at every moment and there is no one to make an act of reparation to remove them." Fr. Robert J. Fox in his book *Fatima Today The Third Millennium*, in describing that 1925 apparition did get it right: "The importance of the First Saturday devotion to the *Immaculate Heart of Mary* cannot be overlooked," he wrote. "Our Lord Himself came to introduce this devotion. His mother then announced it, while exposing her ***Sorrowful and Immaculate Heart!***"

Four years after the apparition in the Convent of Pontevedra, Spain, Lucia received yet another vision in the chapel of the Convent of Tuy also in Spain on June 13, 1929 after she became a nun of the Carmelite Order. This is the description of the vision in her own words: "The whole chapel was illuminated by a supernatural light and a Cross of light appeared above the altar, reaching the ceiling. In a bright light at the upper part of the Cross could be seen the face of a man and His body to the waist (the Father). On His breast was a dove, also of light (the Holy Spirit), and nailed to the Cross was the body of another man (the Son). Somewhat above the waist, I could see a chalice and a large Host suspended in the air onto which drops of blood were falling from the face of Jesus crucified and from the wound in His side. These drops ran down onto the Host and fell into the chalice. Our Lady was beneath the right arm of the Cross. It was *Our Lady of Fatima* with her Heart within a crown of thorns and flames. Under the left arm of the Cross, large letters, as if of crystal clear water, which ran down over the altar, formed the words 'Graces and Mercy.' I understood that it was the Mystery of the Most Holy Trinity which was shown to me." (Indeed, what Sr. Lucia saw and described in this vision was not the *Immaculate Heart* but the *Sorrowful and Immaculate Heart of Mary* "crowned with thorns," standing at the foot of the Cross of the *Man of Sorrows).*

It was not until thirteen years after the apparitions in Fatima ended that on October 13, 1930, the Bishop of Leiria/Fatima, deemed that the miracle and the visions of the children were "worthy of belief." (In the meantime many graces were lost). He declared: "This phenomenon, which no astronomical observatory registered and which therefore was not natural, was witnessed by all categories and by those social classes, believers and non-believers, journalists of the principal Portuguese newspapers, and even by persons some miles away dismissing any explanation of collective illusion."

But as John Haffert wrote, "perhaps what an atomic age should know particularly about this miracle, this really special sign from God to this age, is that the crowd expected to be destroyed. It was suddenly spared." The message is clear. In fact, there is disputably no greater exponent on the Fatima apparitions than John Haffert. In his book *Her Own Words,* he wrote: "In the liturgy of September 15, the feast of *Our Lady of Sorrows,* we are plunged into the mystery of Fatima, *the mystery of Co-redemption.* Fr. A.M. Lepicier says: 'This liturgical emphasis on the Sorrows of Mary, which follows the feast of the Exaltation of the Holy Cross, shows the primordial place given by the Church to Our Lady *in the plan of redemption* and what place she should have in the devotion of Christians redeemed by the Blood of Christ and by the tears of His dear mother.'"

Haffert also wrote: "When Our Lady spoke (on July 13, 1917) of 'several entire nations being *annihilated* if her requests were not heard, can we not hope that instead of a nuclear winter we shall indeed have a nuclear peace? We cannot take back the atomic bomb. We cannot restore into oblivion our knowledge of the power of the atom or the technique of harnessing it into a force sufficiently destructive to wipe out all life on Earth. But everything is possible with God. The miracle of Fatima, so much like a nuclear explosion (which caused all who saw it to think that it was the end of the world), ended in a triumph of faith and joy. At almost the last moment when the crowd at the Cova da Iria on that October 13, 1917 thought the world was about to be destroyed, the great ball of fire gathered back into itself and rose into the sky. Suddenly the sun was shining clearly. The surrounding Earth and even the garments of the people were instantly dried. And to think that this great miracle was performed in the 20th century *'so that everyone may believe!'*"

It is especially noteworthy that whereas the Blessed Virgin did not mention the word "Sorrowful" in Fatima, she appeared as *Our Lady of Sorrows* during the miracle of the sun in October 1917 and that Lucia also saw her with her *Sorrowful and Immaculate Heart* in the convents in 1925 and 1929. In short, the apparitions of Our Lady of Fatima and their messages did not end on October 13, 1917. As explained in the World Apostolate of Fatima's booklet *Sorrowful and Immaculate Heart of Mary*:

"At Fatima Our Blessed Lady asked that her *Immaculate Heart*, that free gift from God's grace, should be specially honoured. But it would not have been in accordance with her perfect humility had she exalted her own merits in proclaiming the glory of her *Sorrowful Heart*. It is therefore incumbent on the faithful, as it were, to complete the message of Fatima by obtaining, through ardent prayer, **the consecration of the world to the *Sorrowful and Immaculate Heart*** of the Mother of our Saviour." Indeed, it is the unsung and ultimate message of Fatima, which has not been appreciated by so many.

But the saga of Fatima did not begin on May 13, 1917 when Her Majesty first appeared to the children. It began in the spring of 1916 when the Angel of Peace (believed to be Michael the Archangel) appeared and said to them: "The Hearts of Jesus and Mary are attentive to the voice of your supplications." Three times did the Angel appear to the children, the third time holding aloft a chalice with a Host suspended above it. From the Host drops of blood fell into the chalice and, leaving them both suspended in mid-air, he prostrated himself on the ground and three times repeated this prayer:

"Most Holy Trinity, Father, Son and Holy Spirit, I adore you profoundly and I offer you the most precious Body, Blood, Soul and Divinity of Jesus Christ, present in all the tabernacles of the world, in reparation for the outrages, sacrileges and indifference by which He Himself is offended. Through the infinite merits of His Most Sacred Heart and the Immaculate Heart of Mary, I beg of you the conversion of poor sinners."

Her Majesty, the Queen of Portugal, then appeared on May 13 of the following year. It was on a Sunday. At that time it was the feast of *Our Lady of the Eucharist,* but on October 13, 1917, she said: *"I am the Lady of the Rosary."* It was all about the dream of Dom Bosco. The Church will be victorious through adoration of the Eucharist and devotion to Our Lady.

Our Lady as she appeared in Fatima. Note the golden star on the hem of her gown.

The apparition of the Sorrowful and Immaculate Heart of Mary beneath the arm of the Cross in the convent in Tuy, Spain.

*The apparition of Mary with the Child
Jesus in the convent in Pontavedra,
Spain.*

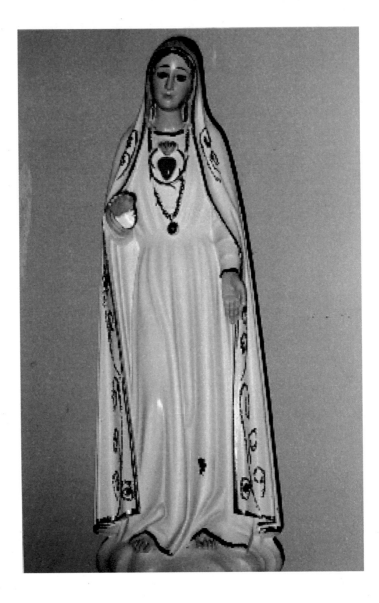

As She appeared under the Cross in Tuy.
The star is still there.

Close-up of the Sorrowful and Immaculate Heart.

Chapter

5

The Column of Smoke

Drs. Michael and Gianna Sullivan of Emmitsburg, Maryland, USA bought a statue in Fatima of the *Sorrowful and Immaculate Heart of Mary* as she appeared to Sr. Lucia in the convent of Tuy in 1929. Soon afterwards the statue was displayed during an open air prayer meeting in Emmitsburg and a distinct "column of black smoke" appeared in front of a photograph of the statue (see page 67). It was a photographic phenomenon. No column of smoke was seen by the congregation. The Sullivans did not understand its significance when they showed me the photo.

Now, in 1988, I took a photograph of the statue of Our Lady of Medjugorje in front of the Church of St. James. It was a bright sunny day when I took a photograph of the statue of the Madonna. Then I took three other photographs in rapid succession. When the film was developed certain unusual phenomena were seen. The first photograph showed the statue of *Our Lady of Medjugorje* against the bright and sunny background with the Crucifix atop the iron railing directly in front of her. The second was a close-up photo of seven roses which I had placed at her feet. The third photograph was most unusual in several aspects. Suddenly, the background was no longer bright and sunny (although the actual day was still quite bright). There was a cloudy haze in the sky and a black *column of smoke* appeared in front of the upper portion of the statue. In the fourth photograph the black *column of smoke* was fully formed, *leaning* obliquely from above the head of the statue down to the arm of the crucified Christ.

I did not understand the significance of this curious imposition on the photograph and thought that perhaps the carrying-cord of the camera had moved in front of the lens. However, several commentators on the photographs did not favour this possibility. Nonetheless, should there be a recurrence and to avoid any possible debate in the future, I cut off the carrying-cord of the camera. I now had, as it were, a bob-tailed camera!

One month later, on October 13, the anniversary of the Virgin's last apparition in Fatima, I was once more in Medjugorje en route to a medical conference in Tanzania and I climbed Krizevac Hill in the cool, early hours of the morning to spend an hour there. Just as I was about to begin the downhill journey to the home of my host Jozo Vasilj, I took a few photographs of the large concrete Cross and the huge copper plaque nearby depicting the fifteenth station of the Cross — the resurrected Christ. What appeared on that print left no doubt that the previous black column seen in front of the statue was not an artifact because coursing across the arm of the huge Cross on Mount Krizevac and *leaning* towards the "resurrected Christ" was a similar black *column of smoke* with a blue tint at its edge, this time horizontally and not vertically.

Seeking an explanation for this *column of smoke,* I experienced an inner call, as it were, to "go to Francis de Sales." In my home library are several books on St. Francis de Sales (1567-1622). He was the founder of the Order of the Visitation nuns and some of the sermons preached by this great Marian Doctor of the Church between 1602 and 1622 were faithfully recorded by the nuns. It was in the first book which I selected from my library, entitled *The Sermons of St. Francis de Sales on Our Lady,* that I found what certainly appeared to be the explanation of the photographic phenomena.

This sermon in the book was given more than four hundred years ago on the feast of the Assumption, August 15, 1602. He started with a quotation from the *Song of Songs,* betraying his well known predilection for a Marian mystical interpretation of Solomon's *Song of Songs.* It was a quotation of Song 8:5: "Who is this coming up from the desert, flowing with delights, *leaning* upon her Lover?" Later on, he quoted another passage: "Who is this coming up from the desert like a *column of smoke,* perfumed with myrrh and frankincense?" (Song 3:6).

Now, according to the Catholic Encyclopedia, Vol. 7, incense, with its sweet-smelling perfume and high-ascending smoke, is typical of prayer which rises up as a pleasing offering in God's sight. Indeed, as prescribed by Yahweh Himself, an altar of incense was positioned directly in front of the curtain which separated the *Holy of Holies* containing the sacred *Ark of the Covenant* from the outer court of the temple. Psalm 141:2 says of incense: "My prayers rise like incense, my hands like the evening sacrifice." In fact, incense is mentioned no less than seventy-five times in the Bible, beginning with the Book of Exodus. There Yahweh said to Moses: *"... Compound an incense, such a blend as the perfumer might make, salted, pure, and holy. Crush a part of it into a fine powder, and put some of this in front of the Testimony (Ark of the Covenant) in the Tent of Meeting, the place appointed for my meeting with you. You must regard it as most holy... You must hold it to be a holy thing reserved for Yahweh"* (Exodus 30:34-37). Incense, therefore, appears to be Yahweh's favourite perfume!

With this background, let us now return to Francis de Sales. Following his quotation from the *Song of Songs*, he began his sermon with this account: "The *Ark of the Covenant* had been kept under tents and pavilions for a very long time when the great King Solomon placed it in the rich and magnificent Temple, which he had prepared for it (1 Kings 8). The rejoicings in Jerusalem were so great at this time that the blood of the sacrifices flowed in the street, *the air was filled with clouds from so much incense and perfume."*

This, therefore, seems to be the explanation for and interpretation of the cloudy haze of the atmosphere, which appeared on the third photograph of *Our Lady of Medjugorje* in the courtyard of the Church of St. James. It was meant to signify the smoke from the incense burnt in front of the (living) *Ark of the* (New) *Covenant,* Our Lady of Medjugorje, another title of Mary.

"But, O God!" St. Francis de Sales continued, "if the reception of that ancient Ark was so solemn, what must we not think to have been that of the new Ark? I speak of the most glorious Virgin Mother of the Son of God on the day of her Assumption. O joy incomprehensible! O feast, full of marvels which makes devout souls, the true daughters of Zion, cry out in admiration: 'Who is this coming up from the desert…?' She comes up from the desert of this lower world, but nevertheless, so perfumed with spiritual gifts, that excluding the Person of her Son, Heaven has nothing comparable. She comes up like a *column of smoke* laden with myrrh, with frankincense: 'Who is this,' it is asked in the *Song of Songs,* 'coming up from the desert like a *column of smoke,* laden with myrrh, frankincense and with the perfume of every exotic dust?'" (Song 3:6).

Francis de Sales added: "But let us look at the remainder of the sentence we have chosen for our subject. It says that this holy Lady coming up from the desert, flowing with delights, is *leaning* upon her Lover … All the saints do the same, and particularly the Virgin. All her perfections, all her virtues, all her happiness are referred, consecrated and dedicated to the glory of her Son, who is their source and their author… If you call her a rose because of her most excellent charity, her colour will only be the blood of her Son. If you say that she is a *column of smoke,* sweet and pleasing, say at once that the fire of this smoke is the charity of her Son; the wood is His Cross. In brief, in all and through all, she is *leaning* upon her Lover."

Indeed, both the great mystic the Venerable Mary of Agreda and the stigmatist and visionary Anne Catherine Emmerich have seen in their visions that Our Lord accompanied His beloved mother when she was bodily assumed into Heaven. In the chapter in the *City of God* on the Assumption of the Blessed Virgin, Mary of Agreda wrote: "Christ our Saviour came back up to Heaven, and at His right hand the Queen, clothed in the gold of variety, was so beautiful that she was the admiration of the heavenly court. All of them turned toward her to look upon her and bless her with songs of praise. Then were heard those mysterious eulogies recorded by Solomon: 'Who is she that comes from the desert like a column of all the aromatic perfumes? Who is she that rises like the aurora, more beautiful than the moon, bright as the sun, terrible as many serried armies? Who is she that comes up from the desert *resting* upon her Beloved and spreading forth abundant delights?"

This then appears to be the reason why the *columns of smoke* in the photographs were obliquely leaning on the arm of the cross. They were meant to be symbolic of Mary *leaning* lovingly on the arm of her beloved Son on the day of her assumption into Heaven. It was a photographic lesson on *Song of Songs* 3:6 and 8:5. It was a signal to the Sullivans and the congregation that it was a depiction of the column of smoke, a well-known Marian symbol, which indeed did appear in the sky in 1917 before Our Lady's apparitions in Fatima. Significantly, the statue was a depiction of the **Sorrowful and Immaculate Heart of Mary**!

In fact, I later discovered that "The column of smoke" is a well-known Marian title and symbol, especially in the Orthodox Church. It is also listed as such in the book *The Dictionary of Mary*.

The first photo taken, close up on the railing. Note the Cross in front of the statue.

***The column of smoke begins to form
against a cloudy background.***

The column of smoke in front of Our Lady and leaning obliquely toward the arm of the Cross.

The column of smoke leaning horizontally toward the arm of the Cross.

The leaning black column of smoke appears in front of the statue of the Sorrowful and Immaculate Heart of Mary owned by the Sullivan family. Note the Cross nearby.

Chapter

6

World War II and September 15

Over the years Berthe Petit's suffering became more and more intense and for the last 35 years of her life she took no earthly nourishment and lived only on the Eucharist. The initiatives taken by Cardinal Mercier of Belgium and Cardinal Bourne of England had eventually faded out and it appeared that the **universal** adoption of the devotion was as far off as ever. In vain, messages were transmitted to Rome but the Vatican remained silent.

Pope Benedict XV died rather suddenly in January 1922 and Pius XI (1922-1939) ascended the Throne of Peter. In that year, four years after the end of World War I, Our Lord said to Berthe: *"The time has not yet arrived. My apostle will arise at the pre-destined hour when the appalling cataclysm which approaches would have upset all the present calculations of mankind and their deplorable policies. My will concerning My Mother's glory will not be fulfilled at present. A period of waiting is still necessary for the work to grow in greatness."*

On September 24, 1924, Our Lord told Berthe: "All the nations are heading toward a frightful cataclysm. I alone can appease the hatred and the discord, and hasten the reign of peace.

I shall do it when My wish for the Heart of My mother will be accomplished. It will come to pass when the hour of despair will strike — an hour toward which everything is moving. Then, in response to the supplications which will ascend to the *Sorrowful and Immaculate Heart* of My mother, I will manifest My power by a miraculous intervention. The whole of Christendom will bow before this triumph which I, as a Son, have determined for My mother."

On December 29, 1930, Our Lady appeared to Berthe and promised her "nothing but suffering". Indeed, on Good Friday of the following year, this "victim soul" had to endure sufferings greater than ever before. That night her lips and tongue bled profusely, the wound in her side opened and the palms of her hands and feet caused her excruciating pain but without opening. In fact, she begged Jesus that she might be able to hide from everyone the marks (stigmata) He deigned to send her.

Pope Pius XI died in 1939 and Eugenio Pacelli was elected Pope on March 3, 1939 at a time of great tension among European states which were preparing for war. He chose the name Pius XII. The government of the Third Reich was far too convinced of its superiority and independence, and saw no need to seek help from anyone, especially the Holy See. While German troops gathered on the Polish border, at 7:00 p.m. on August 24 Pius XII sent a radio message from Castelgandolfo calling on Hitler to negotiation and peace. He said: "The danger is imminent, but there is still time. Nothing is lost with peace; all can be lost with war. Let men return to mutual understanding. Let them begin negotiations anew, conferring with goodwill and with respect for reciprocal rights…"

Having failed in the possibility of a peace conference, on September 1, 1939, as prophesied by Our Lord to Berthe, German troops invaded Poland. Two days later, England declared war on Germany. World War II followed World War I. It was "the ascending curve of preliminary events which will lead to the great manifestation of My justice," as Jesus had foretold on June 29, 1914. Then on January 22, 1940, Berthe heard these words from Jesus: "Belgium will be invaded." On May 10, 1940, German troops broke across the borders of three small states, Belgium, Holland and Denmark. It was on that day that Winston Churchill became the Prime Minister of England.

World War II was by far a more destructive war than World War I and casualties were very high. Germany seemed to be gaining the upper hand when on June 30, 1940, the German General Alfred Jodl, Chief of Operations, wrote: "The final German victory over England is now only a question of time. Enemy offensive operations on a large scale are no longer possible." As William Shirer wrote in his book *The Rise and Fall of the Third Reich,* Hitler's favourite strategist was in a confident and complacent mood. The German Air Force and Navy was to be given the mission of carrying out alone the war against England. It was called Operation Sea Lion and preparations were made for that major assault on England to take place on September 15, 1940.

Then on July 2, 1940, Our Lord repeated: "It is hearts that must be changed. This will only be accomplished by the devotion explained, preached and recommended everywhere. *Devotion to My mother under the title that I wish for her universally is the last help I shall give before the end of time."*

Now, Herman Goering's great air offensive against Britain, Operation Eagle, was first launched on August 15 with the objective of driving the British Air Force from the skies thus achieving the one condition on which the ground landing of the invasion of Britain depended. The Germans had no doubt about victory. Swarms of German bombers and fighters were heading over the Channel towards England. There were 801 bombers and 1,149 fighter planes, but they were mauled by seven squadrons of British Hurricanes and Spitfires. It was the first and largest air battle of that period of the war. It was on the feast of the Assumption of the Blessed Virgin Mary. A wrong choice of day and month by the Germans! It was a recognizable disaster for their Air Force. Goering then called off Operation Eagle entirely, declaring: "It is doubtful whether there is any point in continuing the attacks."

According to William Shirer, it must have been with anxious mind that the German chiefs measured the consequences that this defeat foreboded for the future. The German Air Force, however, still had as their target the port of London, the largest city in the world, which did not require much accuracy to hit. On the late afternoon of Saturday, September 7, 1940, the Germans had begun their first massive bombing of London, carried out by 625 bombers protected by 648 fighters. It was the most devastating attack from the air ever delivered. Vast damage was done on that sprawling city. The assault went on all the following week, night after night, and then, stimulated by it successes, or what it thought were such, the Luftwaffe decided to carry out a great daylight assault on the battered capital.

After two heavy attacks by the Luftwaffe on September

14, this led on Sunday, September 15 to one of the most decisive battles of World War II. Like the great historic Battle of Waterloo, it was on a Sunday. It was on the feast of Our Lady of Sorrows! Some 200 German bombers, escorted by three times as many fighter planes, appeared over the Channel about midday in a daylight attack headed for London. However, the Germans were intercepted by the Royal Air Force before they approached the capital and though some planes got through, many were dispersed and others shot down before they could deliver their bomb load.

Two hours later, an even stronger German formation returned and was again routed. The Royal Air Force shot down 183 for a loss of under 40. That day had shown that the Luftwaffe could not carry out a successful major daylight attack on Britain. That being so, the prospect of an effective landing on English soil by the German army and the navy was dim. September 15 was therefore the turning point, "the crux," as Churchill later judged it, of the Battle of Britain. Two days after that decisive air battle, on September 17, 1940 the Fuehrer called off Operation Sea Lion indefinitely.

Hitler's bomber losses over England had been so severe that they could never have been made up. In fact, the Luftwaffe, as the German confidential records made clear, never fully recovered from the blow it received in the sky over Britain on that September 15. Without their air supremacy, the German army was helpless to move across the narrow Channel waters. Indeed, for the first time in the war Hitler had been stopped, his plans for further conquest frustrated, and just at the moment when he was certain that final victory had been achieved.

Instead, September 15, the feast of Our Lady of Sorrows, was the final death knell for the Luftwaffe. Britain was saved and Churchill told the House of Commons in one of his memorable perorations: "Never in the field of human conflict was so much owed by so many to so few."

On April 25, 1942, Our Lord, alluding to the increase in the tempo of World War II, said to Berthe: "A frightful torment is in preparation. It will be seen that forces launched with much fury will soon be let loose. It is now or never the moment for all of you to give yourself to the *Sorrowful and Immaculate Heart* of My mother. By her acceptance of Calvary My mother has participated in all My sufferings. Devotion to her Heart united to mine will bring **peace**, that true peace so often implored and yet so little merited."

In obedience to this exhortation, Berthe Petit and her friends lost no time in propagating the picture of Our Lady of Ollignies with the invocation so dear to Cardinal Mercier and Cardinal Bourne. These pictures were in a short time widely spread all over Belgium. At the end of 1942, Marian devotions were being widely celebrated to obtain peace, and parishes and religious communities were being consecrated to the *Sorrowful and Immaculate Heart.* However, one day Berthe complained to Jesus: "Lord, how is it that while confiding this work to me, You permit it to be thwarted at every moment?" "You are astonished!" Our Lord answered, "Do you forget that My own acts were constantly thwarted and that My mother always lived in anxiety and with suffering? Remain in your steadfastness in spite of the darkness and give time for the light to make its appearance." "In the hour of triumph," Our Lord also said to

Berthe in 1943, "it will remain clearly manifest that I Myself have inspired in those whom I have freely chosen, a devotion similar to that given to My own Heart. **It is as her Son that I have conceived this devotion for My mother. It is as God that I impose it.**"

Now, like some of the saints, Berthe also sensed the sins of souls and for this reason it was repugnant for her to mix among a crowd. Satan also often tormented her by physical manifestations such as blows so heavy as to provoke a fall, diverse noises and exclamations of hatred. As if that was not sufficient, towards the very end of her long life she experienced the darkness of spiritual dryness and desolation. Not even the feast of Christmas brought her any consolation. However, on the day before she died, speaking of the world consecration to the *Sorrowful and Immaculate Heart of Mary*, she said with a faint smile: **"It will be accomplished."** On March 26, 1943, Berthe breathed her last very peacefully in her sleep. The majesty of her countenance as she laid for three days on her death bed deeply impressed those who came in great numbers to see her.

On May 8, 1945, Field Marshall Keitel signed Germany's final act of capitulation. World War II eventually ended dramatically with the dropping of the atomic bombs first on Hiroshima and then on Nagasaki in August 1945, immediately after which Japan surrendered. It was the beginning of the nuclear era of warfare. It was indeed a "cataclysm." But was it really "*the* appalling cataclysm" about which Our Lord warned?

Chapter

7

Toward the end of World War II

The Blessed Virgin appeared to the children in Fatima towards the end of World War I in 1917, but it is still little known that in the recently-approved apparitions of Our Lady in Amsterdam, Holland, the Queen of Peace appeared to the Dutch visionary Ida Peerdeman just before the end of the World War II on March 25, 1945, the feast of the Annunciation.

Immediately afterwards she showed Ida the Rosary and said: "It is thanks to this." Then Ida saw a large crowd of soldiers many of whom were soldiers of the Allies. She then said: "Now these will soon return to their homes." World War II ended in Europe on May 5, 1945. Significantly, and not by chance, it was the feast day of St. Pope Pius V, who was the Pope who rallied Christians in Europe to storm Heaven with Rosaries before the Battle of Lepanto in 1571.

But why did the Queen choose Amsterdam? During the Middle Ages, Holland was a bastion of Catholicism until 1578 when the Reformation condemned the Catholic religion in Holland to two hundred years of semi-clandestine existence. Yet it was in Amsterdam, the capital city of Holland, that a great Eucharistic miracle took place on March 15, 1345.

On Sunday, February 11, 1951, the anniversary day of

her first apparition to Bernadette Soubirous in Lourdes, Our Lady said to Ida: "I am the Lady, Mother of all Nations. You may say the Lady of all Nations or Mother of all Nations. I have come today precisely in order to tell you that I wish to be known as this. All the children of men of all the countries in the world must be one." It was the cry of her Son to His Father the night before He was crucified: "May they all be one" (John17:21).

On that day she also pleaded that this prayer be said by all: "Lord Jesus Christ, Son of the Father, send now Your Spirit over the earth. Let the Holy Spirit live in the hearts of all nations so that they may be preserved from degeneration, disaster and war. May the *Lady of all Nations*, who once was Mary, be our Advocate. Amen." She then added: "There is a shortage of priests, but of lay people there is no shortage. Let the great movement among the laity be organized…"

She later said to Ida: "My sole purpose is to ensure that the will of the Son is obeyed in these times…The spirit of untruth is making such an appalling progress that it is necessary to act quickly. The whole world is degenerating and for this reason the Son sends the *Lady of all Nations*, who once was Mary… Now I stand an oblation before the Cross for I have suffered with my Son spiritually and, above all, bodily."

She then showed herself standing on a globe in front of the Cross, and said: "The Lady comes standing in front of it as the Son's mother, who with Him has accomplished this work of redemption. 'I am the *Lady of all Nations,* who once was Mary' means that many people have known me just as Mary. Now, however, *in this era*, which is beginning now, I wish to be known as the *Mother of all Nations*. Mankind has been entrusted to the mother. Co-redemptrix I was already at the Annunciation. This means that the mother became the Co-redemptrix by the will of the Father. Never has Miriam or Mary been *officially* called Co-redemptrix. Never has she been *officially* called Mediatrix. Never has she been *officially* called Advocate. These three concepts form one whole. This will be the keystone of Marian history. It will become the dogma of the Co-redemptrix, Mediatrix and Advocate. The other dogmas had to come first. Satan is still the prince of this world. He holds on to everything he can. That then is why the *Lady of all Nations* had to come now, into these times, for she is the Immaculate Conception and, *as a consequence of this*, she is the Co-redemptrix, Mediatrix and Advocate. These three concepts are one." Then she chided: "Is that clearly understood, theologians?"

She later said to Ida: "My prophecy 'from henceforth all generations shall call me blessed' (Luke 1:46:55) will be fulfilled more than ever before once the dogma has been proclaimed... When the dogma, the last dogma in Marian history, has been proclaimed the *Lady of all Nations* will give peace, true peace. I repeat, *true* peace to the world. The nations, however, must say my prayer in union with the Church... Science today has made people forget to show gratitude. They no longer recognize their Creator. Nations, be warned, bow down in deep humility before your Creator... I said a minute ago that alarming inventions would be made. God permits this. But you, nations, can make sure that it does not result in disaster..." How true fifty years later!

The *Lady of all Nations* made many prophecies of a political nature to Ida, including the Korean War and the Vietnam

War long before they occurred. She also prophesied the "Cold War" between the United States and Russia, and warned the United States about possible problems with Formosa (Taiwan). She also foretold the establishment of the state of Israel (which did occur in 1948), the landing of a man on the moon and the conflict in Yugoslavia, among many other prophecies which have already come to pass.

On August 29, 1945, after the end of World War II, Ida wrote in her diary: "I see the Lady standing before me... She refers to a *new, yet strange war* in the distant future which will cause terrible havoc. I predict another great catastrophe for the world." Mostly significant from the point of view of the present-day world conflict (and already experienced by the Kurds in Iraq) was a vision which Ida was shown by the Blessed Virgin. As she wrote in her diary of December 26, 1947: "Now I see something like a cigar or a torpedo flying past me so rapidly that I can scarcely discern it. Its colour seems to be that of aluminum. All of a sudden I see it burst open. I feel with my hand an experience and a number of indefinable sensations. A total loss of sensation! I live and yet I do not live. Then I see before me, swollen faces covered with dreadful ulcers, as it were, a kind of leprosy. Then tiny little black specks are floating around me. I cannot distinguish them with my eyes and it is as if I were made to look at them through something (a microscope). And now I see slides of extraordinary brilliance and upon them those little things enlarge. I do not know how I am to interpret this. 'Bacilli?' I asked. Then the Lady said: 'It is hellish!' I then feel my face swelling and it is swollen when I touch it, all bloated and quite stiff. I can no longer move. Then I hear the Lady again, saying:

'Just think! This is what they are preparing!' Finally the Lady says: 'Nations be warned. It is diabolical. And that is what they are in the process of inventing.'" This was obviously a prophetic vision of germ warfare.

Now, as Ida herself was on occasions concerned that she might be the victim of a deception, she once begged the Blessed Virgin to give her a sign of the authenticity of the apparitions. It was granted. Our Lady prophesied in February 1958 that Pope Pius XII would die at the beginning of October of that year: "The *Lady of all Nations*, the Co-redemptrix, Mediatrix and Advocate," she said to Ida, "will lead him into eternal joy." Pope Pius XII died quite unexpectedly on October 9, 1958. He had held audiences up to a few days previously! She later predicted the death of Pope Paul VI before he died on August 6, 1978. His successor was Albino Luciani, who took the name John Paul I, but he died unexpectedly after 33 days. As Ida was praying that the Holy Spirit would enlighten the minds of the cardinals in a choice of a new Pope, she heard a voice say to her: "He who comes from afar will be Peter's successor." It was repeated on October 16, 1978. That night Ida heard over the radio that the Polish Cardinal Karol Wojtyla was elected Pope. He chose the name Pope John Paul II. He was the first non-Italian Pope for 455 years!

It was on July 17, 1992, that I visited the home and private chapel of Ida Peerdeman in Amsterdam. I chatted a long time with her and then spent one hour in the chapel where the original painting of the *Lady of all Nations* hung at the side of the altar. After fifty years of patience, observations and investigations, and after ensuring that there was no spiritual error in her messages, on May 31, 1996 His Excellency Bishop Hendrik Bomers and Bishop Joseph Maria Punt, Bishops of Haarlem, Amsterdam, gave the *Nihil Obstat* approving the devotion to the *Lady of all Nations*. Then on May 31, 2002, a date Our Lady had previously prophesied, Bishop Punt issued a formal declaration approving the supernatural nature of the apparitions of *Our Lady of all Nations* to Ida Peerdeman.

Now, the Blessed Virgin showed herself to Ida standing in front of the Cross. It was all about her role in salvation history as the mother and companion of the Redeemer. But redemption had to come from suffering. Being just immaculate was not enough. And so, her apparition standing in front of the Cross was a depiction of the **Sorrowful and Immaculate Heart of Mary.** There's the linkage.

The Lady of all Nations

Chapter

8

The Last Help Before the End of Time

"Another great catastrophe for the world." "A strange war." Surely, this must have been the prediction of the new type of warfare which we call international terrorism. It is the world in which we now live more than 50 years after the prophecy was made in Amsterdam by Our Lady. Indeed, the world is on the threshold of a potential major cataclysm and yet so many of us are as complacent about it as were most people in the days of Noah who were "eating and drinking and taking wives and husbands when the flood came" (Matthew 24:38).

The world is at war and the Mother of Mankind has been appearing throughout the centuries, and more frequently in the past two decades, to warn and beseech mankind to return to her Son. As someone once said: "Mankind must put an end to war or war will put an end to mankind." In recent times she and her images have also been seen to weep blood. It is the Rachael of the New Testament weeping for her children "for they are no more."(Matthew 2:18). As a mother she wishes to protect her children from "degeneration, disasters and war" and as little Jacinta of Fatima told Lucia: **"God has entrusted the peace of the world to her."**

Her Son has also been requesting, even before the onset of World War I, that the whole world should be consecrated to the *Sorrowful and Immaculate Heart* of His mother. This title *Sorrowful and Immaculate Heart* is intimately linked with her title **Co-redemptrix**, she who was the co-sufferer and companion of the Redeemer from the crib to the Cross. She was the second Eve who was promised to us in Genesis 3:15.

The first Eve was born from a rib of the first Adam; the second Adam was born from the womb of the second Eve. The first Adam and Eve were disobedient; the second Adam and the second Eve were obedient. The first Eve said "yes" to Satan and sin; the second Eve said "yes" to Gabriel and God. It was a fruit which hung from a tree in the Garden of Eden which was used to introduce sin into the world and enmity between God and man; it was the fruit of the womb of the second Eve, who hung from a tree on Calvary which restored friendship between man and God and brought about the redemption of mankind. The situation was reversed. By the first Eve, death; by the second Eve, life.

The late Fr. Joseph A. Pelletier once wrote: "The co-redemption of Mary is the doctrinal truth expressed by the title *The Sorrowful Heart of Mary* and is what Our Lord wants recognized in the Church on a worldwide basis." And in the messages given to the chosen and holy Berthe Petit, Our Lord repeatedly requested the consecration of the world to the *Sorrowful and Immaculate Heart of Mary*. But as He eventually said to her: **"My apostle will arise at the predestined hour when the appalling cataclysm which approaches would have upset all the present calculations of mankind and their deplorable policies."**

Now, toward the end of World War I, the Mother of Mankind appeared in Fatima in 1917 on the **13th** day of the month from May to October in response to the prayers and pleas of Pope Benedict XV and the Catholic faithful. On July 13, 1917 she warned that "various nations will be annihilated" if her requests for conversion were not heeded. But why did she choose the **13th** day of the month? Little attention has also been paid to the significance of the golden star on the hem of the gown which she wore in her apparitions in Fatima. Indeed, it was the first and only time that she has worn such an ornament. The Old Testament Book of Esther provides the explanation.

The Book of Esther tells of the deliverance of the Jewish nation from annihilation by the intervention of a woman. The Jews were living in exile in Persia after Jerusalem was sacked by the Babylonians but they had many enemies there. At that time the singular beauty of Esther, a Jewess, attracted Ahasuerus, the King of Persia (485-465 BC), and she was taken into his palace to succeed Vashti as queen. The king, however, did not know that she was Jewish.

The Book records that Haman, a high official in the king's administration, akin to a Prime Minister, had resolved to wipe all the members of the Jewish race throughout the empire of Persia. The date chosen by lot for this extermination was the 13th day of the month. In fact, Haman has been described by modern Jewish writers as an Old Testament Hitler, manifesting an intense hatred for the Jews. He succeeded in convincing the king of the necessity for the extermination of the Jews and the decree was signed in the name of King Ahasuerus, sealed with his ring and letters were sent by couriers to every province of the realm ordering the destruction, slaughter and annihilation of all the Jews, the young and old, women and children. It was to be done on the **13th** day of the month.

When Queen Esther's maids told her about it, she was totally overcome with grief. She then sent an urgent message to her step-father Mordecai, a fellow Jew and Benjamite, who held a high position in government, but who was also hated by Haman. She said to him: "Go and assemble all the Jews now in Susa (the capital city of Persia) and fast for me. Do not eat or drink day and night for three days. For my part, I and my maids would keep the same fast after which I shall go to the king in spite of the law, and if I perish, I perish."

On the third day, when she had finished praying and fasting, she took off her mourning attire and dressed herself in her full splendour. Radiant as she was, she then appeared in the presence of the king, who was so impressed by her beauty and her courage that he rescinded the order and Haman was the one who was hanged. The Jews were also allowed to avenge themselves on the guilty Persians who plotted against them. The King's command and decree came into force on the **13**[th] day of the month (Esther 13:7,9:15-32).

And so, it is interesting that over two millennia later, on April 13-14, 2006, Mahmoud Ahmadinejad, the new President of Iran, called for the annihilation of Israel (to be "wiped from the face of the earth"). Now, for two and half centuries from its founding in the sixth century BC until its conquest by Alexander the Great in the fourth century BC, Persia was the dominant power of the ancient world. They held at bay the empire of Rome and Byzantine for over 700 years before finally succumbing to the rising power of Islam in the middle of the seventh century AD. However, its name was changed to Iran since 1935. And so, it appears that Persian history is repeating itself!

On October 13, the miracle of the sun took place and when the 70,000 spectators in the Cova da Iria in Fatima saw the sun leave its celestial abode and came hurling down to Earth, they all thought that they were going to perish. However, as the little visionaries saw, with a signal of her right hand the Queen, as it were, commanded the sun to return to its celestial position and symbolically saved the crowd from instant annihilation. But what we did not know in 1917, we now know.

Science has since discovered that the sun has a huge nuclear reactor in its core (like all the other stars), continually converting hydrogen into helium. It is this nuclear conversion process which is now used in the making of hydrogen bombs! She came to Fatima, among other things, warning of the possible annihilation of nations but it is only nuclear bombs which can annihilate nations. She wore a golden star on the hem of her gown. It was her calling card. Gold is the regal colour and "Esther" means "Star." In short, Her Majesty came to Fatima in 1917 as the "Esther of the New Testament" to save her children from annihilation.

When she gave birth to the Prince of Peace, she became the Queen of Peace. She is indeed the Queen of Peace. In World War II the United States entered the war on December 8, 1942. It was an entry which won the day for the Allies and saved the world from Hitlerian domination. World War II ended on August 15, 1945 with the surrender of Japan. It was on the feast of the Assumption of the Blessed Virgin Mary. Six years later, Japan signed another formal pact in San Francisco pertaining to its surrender. It was called the Second World War Peace Treaty. It was on September 8, 1951, the feast of the Nativity of the Blessed Virgin Mary. The signing of the Intermediate Range Nuclear Forces Treaty in Washington by Mikhail Gorbachev and Ronald Reagan abolishing medium range missiles in Europe took place on December 8, 1987, the feast of the Immaculate Conception. The 70-year reign of the atheistic Communistic Party in Russia suddenly and unexpectedly collapsed on August 22, 1991. It was the feast of the Queenship of Mary. The Communist flag was taken down for the last time over the Kremlin on December 25, 1990. It was the day we celebrate the birth of her Son. One year later, once more on Christmas day, Communism was declared illegal in Russia. And all this is so little known and appreciated.

Now, it was Germany which started World War I and World War II. Belgium was the first country to be invaded when Germany violated its neutrality. Is this perhaps why Our Lord, as a matter of protocol, chose Berthe Petit of Belgium to give his first messages about the *Sorrowful and Immaculate Heart* of His mother, the Queen of Peace? Lenin led the Russian revolution in 1917, which gave birth to atheistic communism. Catholic Poland was the first country to be attacked militarily by Germany in World War II and it is possibly of relevant significance in this era and in the plan of God that the Pole, Karol Wojtyla, was the first elected non-Italian Pope in 455 years!

Pope Benedict XV was called the "Pope of the Peace" in World War I. Ninety years later, on April 19, 2005, following the death of the great Polish Pope John Paul II, the German Cardinal Joseph Ratzinger was elected Pope. Significantly, he chose the

BENEDICT XV
1914 - 1922

BENEDICT XVI
2005 -

name Benedict XVI. As Prof Klaus Berger, a theologian in Germany's Heidelberg University, wrote in the magazine *Inside the Vatican* of January 2006: "The last time Germany played a major role in the history of the Church was about 500 years ago — as the country where the Reformation was born (through Martin Luther), that Reformation which split Europe into two: Protestant north and Catholic south. The German Pope does not only come from where the Reformation was born. Karl Marx also came from this country. But it is also the country where the great medieval theologian St. Albert the Great was born!

"My apostle would arise at the predestined hour when the appalling cataclysm which approaches will have upset all the present calculations of mankind and their deplorable policies," so prophesied Our Lord to Berthe Petit. However, that apostle will have to be a Pope or someone in the hierarchy of the Church who can influence the Holy Father to consecrate the world to the *Sorrowful and Immaculate Heart of Mary* since only a Pope can consecrate the world or define a Marian dogma.

This German Pope has made a historic visit to Auschwitz where he ardently prayed for the victims of Nazi Germany. And so, I end this book by asking our new Pope from Germany: "Are you not, in God's providential plan and in the spirit of your model, Pope Benedict XV, also the chosen "apostle" to usher in an era of peace by consecrating the world to the *Sorrowful and Immaculate Heart of Mary* and in so doing save the world from the "cataclysm" of a World War III?" According to Berthe Petit, it is said to be the last help before the end of time. If this is so, as I believe it to be, then this book may well be considered to be *the* most important book of this era.

Sorrowful and Immaculate Heart of Mary, pray for us.

Personal Consecration

Composed by Berthe Petit

Sorrowful and Immaculate Heart of Mary, dwelling pure and holy, cover my soul with your maternal protection so that being ever faithful to the voice of Jesus, it responds to His and obeys His Divine Will.

I wish, O, my mother, to keep increasingly before me your co-redemption in order to live intimately with your Heart that is totally united to the Heart of your Divine Son.

Fasten me to this Heart by your own virtues and sorrows. Protect me always.

Also by Professor Courtenay Bartholomew

A Scientist Researches Mary, Ark of the Covenant

A Scientist Researches Mary, Mother and Co-Redemptrix

A Scientist Researches Mary, Mother of all Nations

Her Majesty Mary, Queen of Peace

The Immaculate Heart of Mary,
Jesus Eucharist and
Mother Seton's Emmitsburg

The Passion of the Christ and His Mother